W9-BKE-916

Jumping Spiders

ABDO
Publishing Company

A Buddy Book

by

Julie Murray

VISIT US AT
www.abdopub.com

Published by Buddy Books, an imprint of ABDO Publishing Company, 4940 Viking Drive, Suite 622, Edina, Minnesota 55435. Copyright © 2005 by Abdo Consulting Group, Inc. International copyrights reserved in all countries. No part of this book may be reproduced in any form without written permission from the publisher.

Printed in the United States.

Edited by: Christy DeVillier
Contributing Editors: Matt Ray, Michael P. Goecke
Graphic Design: Maria Hosley
Image Research: Deborah Coldiron
Photographs: Mark Kostich, Minden Pictures, Photodisc

Library of Congress Cataloging-in-Publication Data

Murray, Julie, 1969-
  Jumping spiders / Julie Murray.
      p. cm. — (Animal kingdom)
  Includes bibliographical references (p.) and index.
  Contents: Spiders — Jumping spiders — Size and colors — Their bodies — Where they live — Senses/defenses — Communication — Food — Babies.
  ISBN 1-59197-323-6
      1. Jumping spiders—Juvenile literature. [1. Jumping spiders. 2. Spiders.] I. Title.

QL458.42.S24M87 2004
595.4'4—dc22

                                        2003061676

Contents

Arachnids

There are more than 35,000 kinds of spiders. Spiders are **arachnids**. Scorpions and ticks are arachnids, too.

Spiders are arachnids.

How are **arachnids** different from insects? Insects have three main body parts. Arachnids have two main body parts. Insects have six legs. Arachnids have eight legs. Some insects have wings. Arachnids do not have wings.

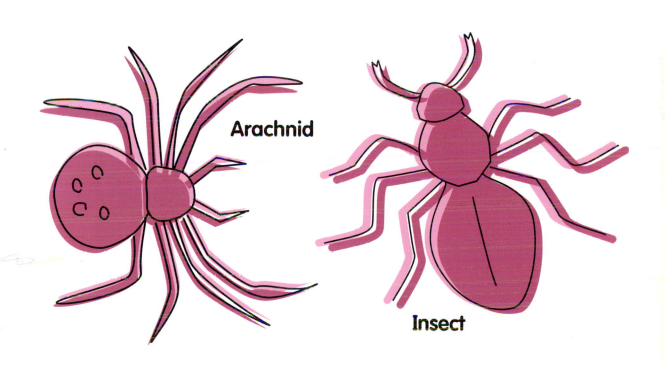

Arachnid

Insect

Jumping Spiders

Jumping spiders are the largest spider family. There are more than 4,000 different kinds of jumping spiders.

Jumping spiders are named for their great jumping skills. They can jump more than 40 times the length of their body. This is equal to a six-foot-tall (two-meter-tall) person jumping 240 feet (73 m) in one leap!

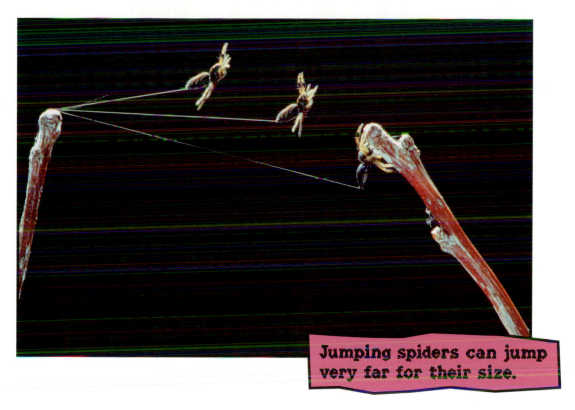

Jumping spiders can jump very far for their size.

Jumping spiders do not have a harmful bite. Some people keep them as pets. These spiders will jump onto someone's outstretched finger. They are not afraid of people.

Size And Color

Jumping spiders are small. Most adults are less than one inch (three cm) long. They are covered with thick hair.

Jumping spiders are colorful. They can be red, yellow, orange, green, purple, blue, or silver. Many male jumping spiders have beautiful colors and patterns. Females are commonly less colorful.

Jumping spiders are small and colorful.

Body Parts

Like all **arachnids**, jumping spiders have two main body parts. The front part is the **cephalothorax**. The spider's eyes, brain, mouth, and stomach are in the cephalothorax.

The spider's back part is called the **abdomen**. Its heart and lungs are inside the abdomen. On the tip of the abdomen are the spider's **spinnerets**. Silk thread comes from the spinnerets.

Jumping spiders have eight short legs. Each leg has seven joints. Joints allow the spider's legs to bend.

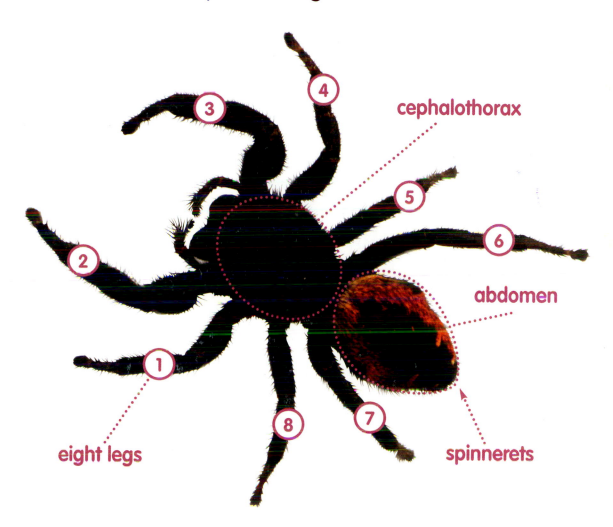

cephalothorax

abdomen

spinnerets

eight legs

Where They Live

Jumping spiders live all over the world. They can live in warm places or cold places. About 300 kinds live in the United States and Canada. Jumping spiders live in South America, Europe, Asia, and Australia, too.

Jumping spiders like sunshine. They are active during the day.

Jumping spiders build special nests with the silk threads from their **spinnerets**. Their nests are often in hidden places and have a narrow opening. They go to their nest to hide or sleep. Some jumping spiders **hibernate** in their nest during the winter.

A common nesting place for jumping spiders is under rocks.

Hunting And Eating

Jumping spiders eat flies, beetles, butterflies, crickets, and other insects. They also eat other spiders.

Jumping spiders do not build webs to trap food. Instead, they hunt. Jumping spiders quietly sneak up behind **prey**. Then, they leap onto prey and kill it.

This jumping spider has caught an ant.

Catching a flying insect is tricky. Before jumping, a jumping spider sends out a silk thread. This sticky thread is the spider's lifeline. It stays attached to the spider and to something else. The thread holds the spider as it leaps into the air.

Keen Eyesight

The jumping spider has very good eyesight. It has four large eyes on its face. Four smaller eyes are on top of its head. Keen eyesight helps jumping spiders hunt **prey**.

Guarding Against Enemies

Birds, snakes, and other animals eat spiders. Jumping spiders often run away from these **predators**.

Spiders must guard against spider-eating snakes and birds.

Camouflage is another way jumping spiders guard against danger. Some have colors that match their surroundings. This makes it harder for **predators** to find them.

Looking like an ant helps the spear-jawed jumping spider hide from predators.

Courtship Dances

Male jumping spiders are often looking for mates. When he finds a female, the male spider dances for

her. Each kind of jumping spider has its own dance. He may move side to side. He may wave his colorful legs or jump up and down.

Spiderlings

Spring and summer is a common time for female jumping spiders to lay eggs. They lay their eggs in a special eggsac. This eggsac keeps the eggs safe. The mother stays near to watch over the eggs.

A mother jumping spider and her eggs.

Baby spiders are called spiderlings. The spiderlings stay inside the eggsac after hatching. There, the spiderlings can grow bigger. After many weeks the young spiders leave the eggsac.

Important Words

abdomen the back part of a spider's body.

arachnids small animals with two body parts and eight legs.

camouflage when an animal's coloring matches its surroundings. Camouflage helps animals hide from predators.

cephalothorax the front part of a spider's body.

hibernate to sleep during the winter months.

predator an animal that hunts and eats other animals.

prey an animal that is food for other animals.

spinneret the part of the spider's body that makes silk.

Web Sites

To learn more about jumping spiders, visit ABDO Publishing Company on the World Wide Web. Web sites about jumping spiders are featured on our Book Links page. These links are routinely monitored and updated to provide the most current information available.

www.abdopub.com

Index